A Daily Planner

Managing
ALL YOUR DAYS
Effectively

I0G91148

Activinotes

Activinotes

DAILY JOURNALS, PLANNERS, NOTEBOOKS AND OTHER BLANK BOOKS

DAILY PLANNERS

DATE

M	T	W	T	F	S	S

Inspiration

_____

_____

_____

_____

general plan

_____

_____

_____

_____

_____

_____

_____

_____

_____

_____

to do list

to go

contact

Note

_____

_____

_____

_____

_____

_____

_____

_____

DAILY PLANNERS

DATE

M T W T F S S

Inspiration

_____

_____

_____

_____

general plan	to do list

○ _____

○ _____   **to go**

○ _____

○ _____

○ _____

○ _____

○ _____

○ _____   **contact**

○ _____

○ _____

○ _____

Note

_____

_____

_____

_____

_____

_____

_____

DAILY PLANNERS

DATE

M T W T F S S

Inspiration

_____

_____

_____

_____

general plan	to do list

to go

contact

Note

_____

_____

_____

_____

_____

_____

_____

DAILY PLANNERS

DATE

M T W T F S S

Inspiration

_____

_____

_____

_____

general plan	to do list	

to go

contact

Note

_____

_____

_____

_____

_____

_____

_____

_____

DAILY PLANNERS

DATE

M	T	W	T	F	S	S

Inspiration

_____

_____

_____

general plan	to do list

_____ ◯ _____

_____ ◯ _____   **to go**

_____ ◯ _____

_____ ◯ _____

_____ ◯ _____

_____ ◯ _____

_____ ◯ _____   **contact**

_____ ◯ _____

_____ ◯ _____

_____ ◯ _____

_____ ◯ _____

Note

_____

_____

_____

_____

_____

_____

_____

DAILY PLANNERS

DATE

M	T	W	T	F	S	S

Inspiration

_____

_____

_____

_____

general plan	to do list	

○ _____

○ _____   **to go**

○ _____

○ _____

○ _____

○ _____

○ _____

○ _____   **contact**

○ _____

○ _____

○ _____

Note

_____

_____

_____

_____

_____

_____

DAILY PLANNERS

DATE

M	T	W	T	F	S	S

Inspiration

general plan   to do list

to go

contact

Note

DAILY PLANNERS

DATE

M	T	W	T	F	S	S

Inspiration

general plan   to do list

to go

contact

Note

DAILY PLANNERS

DATE

M	T	W	T	F	S	S

Inspiration

_____

_____

_____

general plan	to do list	

to go

contact

Note

_____

_____

_____

_____

_____

_____

_____

DAILY PLANNERS

DATE

M	T	W	T	F	S	S

Inspiration

_____

_____

_____

_____

general plan	to do list

to go

contact

Note

_____

_____

_____

_____

_____

_____

_____

DAILY PLANNERS

DATE

M	T	W	T	F	S	S

Inspiration

_____

_____

_____

_____

general plan	to do list	

_____

_____

_____

_____

_____

_____

_____

_____

_____

_____

to go

contact

Note

_____

_____

_____

_____

_____

_____

_____

DAILY PLANNERS

DATE

M	T	W	T	F	S	S

Inspiration

_____
_____
_____
_____

general plan   to do list

_____   ○ _____
_____   ○ _____   **to go**
_____   ○ _____
_____   ○ _____
_____   ○ _____
_____   ○ _____
_____   ○ _____   **contact**
_____   ○ _____
_____   ○ _____
_____   ○ _____
_____   ○ _____

Note

_____
_____
_____
_____
_____
_____
_____

DAILY PLANNERS

DATE

M	T	W	T	F	S	S

Inspiration

_____

_____

_____

_____

general plan	to do list	

_____ ○ _____

_____ ○ _____   **to go**

_____ ○ _____

_____ ○ _____

_____ ○ _____

_____ ○ _____

_____ ○ _____   **contact**

_____ ○ _____

_____ ○ _____

_____ ○ _____

_____ ○ _____

Note

_____

_____

_____

_____

_____

_____

_____

DAILY PLANNERS

DATE

M T W T F S S

Inspiration

_____

_____

_____

_____

general plan	to do list

to go

contact

Note

_____

_____

_____

_____

_____

_____

_____

DAILY PLANNERS

DATE

M T W T F S S

Inspiration

_____
_____
_____
_____

general plan   to do list

○
○   **to go**
○
○
○
○
○
○   **contact**
○
○
○

Note

_____
_____
_____
_____
_____
_____
_____

DAILY PLANNERS

DATE

M	T	W	T	F	S	S

Inspiration

_____

_____

_____

_____

general plan	to do list	

to go

contact

Note

_____

_____

_____

_____

_____

_____

_____

_____

DAILY PLANNERS

DATE

M T W T F S S

Inspiration

_____

_____

_____

general plan	to do list	

to go

contact

Note

_____

_____

_____

_____

_____

_____

_____

DAILY PLANNERS

DATE

M T W T F S S

Inspiration

_____

_____

_____

_____

general plan	to do list

○ _____

○ _____ **to go**

○ _____

○ _____

○ _____

○ _____

○ _____

○ _____ **contact**

○ _____

○ _____

○ _____

Note

_____

_____

_____

_____

_____

_____

_____

_____

DAILY PLANNERS

DATE

M T W T F S S

Inspiration

_____
_____
_____
_____

general plan   to do list

_____   **to go**
_____ ◯
_____ ◯
_____ ◯
_____ ◯
_____ ◯
_____ ◯   **contact**
_____ ◯
_____ ◯
_____ ◯
_____ ◯

Note

_____
_____
_____
_____
_____
_____
_____

DAILY PLANNERS

DATE

| | | | | | | |
|M|T|W|T|F|S|S|

Inspiration

_____

_____

_____

_____

general plan	to do list	

to go

contact

Note

_____

_____

_____

_____

_____

_____

_____

DAILY PLANNERS

DATE

M	T	W	T	F	S	S

Inspiration

_____

_____

_____

_____

general plan	to do list	

to go

contact

Note

_____

_____

_____

_____

_____

_____

_____

DAILY PLANNERS

DATE

M	T	W	T	F	S	S

Inspiration

_____

_____

_____

general plan	to do list

to go

contact

Note

_____

_____

_____

_____

_____

_____

_____

DAILY PLANNERS

DATE

| | | | | | | |
|M|T|W|T|F|S|S|

Inspiration

_____

_____

_____

_____

general plan	to do list

to go

○
○
○
○
○
○
○
○
○
○
○

contact

Note

_____

_____

_____

_____

_____

_____

_____

DAILY PLANNERS

DATE

M	T	W	T	F	S	S

Inspiration

_____

_____

_____

_____

general plan	to do list	

to go

contact

Note

_____

_____

_____

_____

_____

_____

_____

DAILY PLANNERS

DATE

M	T	W	T	F	S	S

Inspiration

_____

_____

_____

_____

general plan	to do list

to go

contact

Note

_____

_____

_____

_____

_____

_____

_____

_____

DAILY PLANNERS

DATE

M	T	W	T	F	S	S

Inspiration

_____

_____

_____

_____

general plan	to do list	

to go

contact

Note

_____

_____

_____

_____

_____

_____

_____

_____

DAILY PLANNERS

DATE

M T W T F S S

Inspiration

_____

_____

_____

_____

general plan	to do list	

○ _____

○ _____   **to go**

○ _____

○ _____

○ _____

○ _____

○ _____

○ _____   **contact**

○ _____

○ _____

○ _____

Note

_____

_____

_____

_____

_____

_____

_____

_____

DAILY PLANNERS

DATE

M	T	W	T	F	S	S

Inspiration

_____

_____

_____

_____

general plan	to do list

to go

contact

Note

_____

_____

_____

_____

_____

_____

_____

_____

DAILY PLANNERS

DATE

M	T	W	T	F	S	S

Inspiration

_____

_____

_____

_____

general plan	to do list	

○ _____

○ _____

○ _____   **to go**

○ _____

○ _____

○ _____

○ _____

○ _____   **contact**

○ _____

○ _____

○ _____

Note

_____

_____

_____

_____

_____

_____

_____

DAILY PLANNERS

DATE

M	T	W	T	F	S	S

Inspiration

_____

_____

_____

_____

general plan	to do list	

to go

contact

Note

_____

_____

_____

_____

_____

_____

_____

_____

DAILY PLANNERS

DATE

M T W T F S S

Inspiration

_____

_____

_____

general plan	to do list	

○ _____

○ _____

○ _____   **to go**

○ _____

○ _____

○ _____

○ _____

○ _____   **contact**

○ _____

○ _____

○ _____

Note

_____

_____

_____

_____

_____

_____

_____

DAILY PLANNERS

DATE

M T W T F S S

Inspiration

_____

_____

_____

_____

general plan	to do list	

to go

contact

Note

_____

_____

_____

_____

_____

_____

_____

_____

DAILY PLANNERS

DATE

M	T	W	T	F	S	S

Inspiration
_____
_____
_____
_____

general plan	to do list

_____
_____   ○
_____   ○   **to go**
_____   ○
_____   ○
_____   ○
_____   ○
_____   ○
_____   ○   **contact**
_____   ○
_____   ○
_____   ○

Note
_____
_____
_____
_____
_____
_____
_____
_____

DAILY PLANNERS

DATE

M T W T F S S

Inspiration

_____

_____

_____

_____

general plan	to do list

to go

contact

Note

_____

_____

_____

_____

_____

_____

_____

DAILY PLANNERS

DATE

M T W T F S S

Inspiration

_____

_____

_____

general plan	to do list

to go

contact

Note

_____

_____

_____

_____

_____

_____

_____

DAILY PLANNERS

DATE

M	T	W	T	F	S	S

Inspiration

_____

_____

_____

_____

general plan	to do list

○
○
○
○
○
○
○
○
○
○
○

to go

contact

Note

_____

_____

_____

_____

_____

_____

_____

DAILY PLANNERS

DATE

M	T	W	T	F	S	S

Inspiration

_____

_____

_____

_____

general plan	to do list

to go

contact

Note

_____

_____

_____

_____

_____

_____

_____

DAILY PLANNERS

DATE

M	T	W	T	F	S	S

Inspiration

_____

_____

_____

_____

general plan	to do list	

to go

contact

Note

_____

_____

_____

_____

_____

_____

_____

_____

DAILY PLANNERS

DATE

M	T	W	T	F	S	S

Inspiration

_____

_____

_____

_____

general plan	to do list	

to go

contact

Note

_____

_____

_____

_____

_____

_____

_____

DAILY PLANNERS

DATE

M T W T F S S

Inspiration

_____
_____
_____
_____

general plan	to do list

to go

contact

Note

_____
_____
_____
_____
_____
_____
_____
_____

DAILY PLANNERS

DATE

M T W T F S S

Inspiration

_____

_____

_____

_____

general plan	to do list

○ _____

○ _____

○ _____   **to go**

○ _____

○ _____

○ _____

○ _____

○ _____   **contact**

○ _____

○ _____

○ _____

Note

_____

_____

_____

_____

_____

_____

_____

_____

DAILY PLANNERS

DATE

M	T	W	T	F	S	S

Inspiration

_____

_____

_____

_____

general plan	to do list

to go

contact

Note

_____

_____

_____

_____

_____

_____

_____

DAILY PLANNERS

DATE

M	T	W	T	F	S	S

Inspiration

_____

_____

_____

_____

general plan	to do list

to go

contact

Note

_____

_____

_____

_____

_____

_____

_____

DAILY PLANNERS

DATE

M T W T F S S

Inspiration

_____
_____
_____
_____

general plan	to do list	

○ _____
○ _____
○ _____
○ _____
○ _____
○ _____
○ _____
○ _____
○ _____
○ _____
○ _____

to go

contact

Note

_____
_____
_____
_____
_____
_____
_____

DAILY PLANNERS

DATE

M	T	W	T	F	S	S

Inspiration

_____

_____

_____

_____

general plan	to do list	

_____ ○ _____ **to go**

_____ ○ _____

_____ ○ _____

_____ ○ _____

_____ ○ _____

_____ ○ _____

_____ ○ _____ **contact**

_____ ○ _____

_____ ○ _____

_____ ○ _____

_____ ○ _____

Note

_____

_____

_____

_____

_____

_____

_____

DAILY PLANNERS

DATE

M	T	W	T	F	S	S

Inspiration

_____

_____

_____

_____

general plan   to do list

to go

contact

Note

_____

_____

_____

_____

_____

_____

_____

_____

DAILY PLANNERS

DATE

M	T	W	T	F	S	S

Inspiration

general plan   to do list

to go

contact

Note

DAILY PLANNERS

DATE

M T W T F S S

Inspiration

_____

_____

_____

_____

general plan	to do list

to go

contact

Note

_____

_____

_____

_____

_____

_____

_____

DAILY PLANNERS

DATE

M	T	W	T	F	S	S

Inspiration

_____

_____

_____

_____

general plan	to do list	

to go

contact

Note

_____

_____

_____

_____

_____

_____

_____

_____

DAILY PLANNERS

DATE

M	T	W	T	F	S	S

Inspiration

_____

_____

_____

_____

general plan	to do list	

⭕ _____
⭕ _____
⭕ _____
⭕ _____
⭕ _____
⭕ _____
⭕ _____
⭕ _____
⭕ _____
⭕ _____
⭕ _____

to go

contact

Note

_____

_____

_____

_____

_____

_____

_____

DAILY PLANNERS

DATE

☐☐☐☐☐☐☐

M T W T F S S

Inspiration

_____

_____

_____

_____

general plan	to do list

to go

contact

Note

_____

_____

_____

_____

_____

_____

_____

DAILY PLANNERS

DATE

M T W T F S S

Inspiration

_____

_____

_____

_____

general plan   to do list

to go

contact

Note

_____

_____

_____

_____

_____

_____

_____

_____

DAILY PLANNERS

DATE

M T W T F S S

Inspiration

_____

_____

_____

| general plan | to do list |

to go

contact

Note

_____

_____

_____

_____

_____

_____

_____

DAILY PLANNERS

DATE

M T W T F S S

Inspiration
_____
_____
_____
_____

general plan	to do list

general plan

to do list

to go

contact

Note
_____
_____
_____
_____
_____
_____
_____
_____

DAILY PLANNERS

DATE

M	T	W	T	F	S	S

Inspiration

_____

_____

_____

_____

general plan	to do list

to go

contact

Note

_____

_____

_____

_____

_____

_____

_____

DAILY PLANNERS

DATE

M	T	W	T	F	S	S

Inspiration

general plan   to do list

to go

contact

Note

DAILY PLANNERS

DATE

M	T	W	T	F	S	S

Inspiration

_____

_____

_____

_____

general plan	to do list	

to go

contact

Note

_____

_____

_____

_____

_____

_____

_____

_____

DAILY PLANNERS

DATE

M	T	W	T	F	S	S

Inspiration

_____

_____

_____

_____

general plan	to do list	

to go

contact

Note

_____

_____

_____

_____

_____

_____

_____

_____

DAILY PLANNERS

DATE

M	T	W	T	F	S	S

Inspiration

_____

_____

_____

_____

general plan	to do list

to go

contact

Note

_____

_____

_____

_____

_____

_____

_____

DAILY PLANNERS

DATE

M	T	W	T	F	S	S

Inspiration

_____

_____

_____

_____

general plan	to do list

to go

contact

Note

_____

_____

_____

_____

_____

_____

_____

DAILY PLANNERS

DATE

M T W T F S S

Inspiration

_____

_____

_____

_____

general plan	to do list	

○ _____

○ _____

○ _____   **to go**

○ _____

○ _____

○ _____

○ _____   **contact**

○ _____

○ _____

○ _____

○ _____

Note

_____

_____

_____

_____

_____

_____

DAILY PLANNERS

DATE

M T W T F S S

Inspiration

_____

_____

_____

_____

general plan	to do list	

○ _____
○ _____
○ _____   **to go**
○ _____
○ _____
○ _____
○ _____
○ _____
○ _____   **contact**
○ _____
○ _____

Note

_____

_____

_____

_____

_____

_____

_____

DAILY PLANNERS

DATE

M	T	W	T	F	S	S

Inspiration

_____

_____

_____

_____

general plan	to do list	

to go

contact

Note

_____

_____

_____

_____

_____

_____

_____

DAILY PLANNERS

DATE

M	T	W	T	F	S	S

Inspiration

_____

_____

_____

_____

general plan	to do list	

to go

contact

Note

_____

_____

_____

_____

_____

_____

_____

DAILY PLANNERS

DATE

M T W T F S S

Inspiration

_____

_____

_____

_____

general plan	to do list

_____

_____

_____

_____

_____

_____

_____

_____

_____

_____

to go

contact

Note

_____

_____

_____

_____

_____

_____

_____

DAILY PLANNERS

DATE

M	T	W	T	F	S	S

Inspiration

_____

_____

_____

_____

general plan	to do list	

to go

contact

Note

_____

_____

_____

_____

_____

_____

_____

DAILY PLANNERS

DATE

M T W T F S S

Inspiration

_____
_____
_____
_____

general plan	to do list

to go

contact

Note

_____
_____
_____
_____
_____
_____
_____
_____

DAILY PLANNERS

DATE

M T W T F S S

Inspiration

general plan   to do list

○
○
○
○
○
○
○
○
○
○

to go

contact

Note

DAILY PLANNERS

DATE

M	T	W	T	F	S	S

Inspiration
_____
_____
_____
_____

general plan	to do list	

to go

contact

Note
_____
_____
_____
_____
_____
_____
_____

DAILY PLANNERS

DATE

M	T	W	T	F	S	S

Inspiration

_____

_____

_____

_____

general plan	to do list	

○ _____ **to go**

○ _____

○ _____

○ _____

○ _____

○ _____

○ _____ **contact**

○ _____

○ _____

○ _____

Note

_____

_____

_____

_____

_____

_____

_____

DAILY PLANNERS

DATE

M	T	W	T	F	S	S

Inspiration

general plan   to do list

to go

contact

Note

DAILY PLANNERS

DATE

M	T	W	T	F	S	S

Inspiration

_____
_____
_____
_____

general plan	to do list	

_____ ○ _____ **to go**
_____ ○ _____
_____ ○ _____
_____ ○ _____
_____ ○ _____
_____ ○ _____
_____ ○ _____ **contact**
_____ ○ _____
_____ ○ _____
_____ ○ _____
_____ ○ _____

Note

_____
_____
_____
_____
_____
_____
_____
_____

DAILY PLANNERS

DATE

M	T	W	T	F	S	S

Inspiration

_____

_____

_____

_____

general plan	to do list	

to go

contact

Note

_____

_____

_____

_____

_____

_____

DAILY PLANNERS

DATE

M T W T F S S

Inspiration

general plan   to do list

to go

contact

Note

DAILY PLANNERS

DATE

M T W T F S S

Inspiration
_____
_____
_____
_____

general plan	to do list

_____ ○
_____ ○   **to go**
_____ ○
_____ ○
_____ ○
_____ ○
_____ ○
_____ ○   **contact**
_____ ○
_____ ○
_____ ○

Note
_____
_____
_____
_____
_____
_____
_____

DAILY PLANNERS

DATE

M	T	W	T	F	S	S

Inspiration

general plan   to do list

to go

contact

Note

DAILY PLANNERS

DATE

M	T	W	T	F	S	S

Inspiration

_____

_____

_____

_____

general plan	to do list

to go

contact

Note

_____

_____

_____

_____

_____

_____

_____

DAILY PLANNERS

DATE

M T W T F S S

Inspiration
_____
_____
_____
_____

general plan	to do list

to go

contact

Note
_____
_____
_____
_____
_____
_____
_____

DAILY PLANNERS

DATE

M	T	W	T	F	S	S

Inspiration

_____

_____

_____

general plan	to do list	

to go

contact

Note

_____

_____

_____

_____

_____

_____

_____

_____

DAILY PLANNERS

DATE

M T W T F S S

Inspiration

general plan   to do list

to go

contact

Note

DAILY PLANNERS

DATE

M	T	W	T	F	S	S

Inspiration

_____

_____

_____

_____

general plan	to do list

to go

contact

Note

_____

_____

_____

_____

_____

_____

_____

_____

DAILY PLANNERS

DATE

M T W T F S S

Inspiration

_____

_____

_____

_____

general plan	to do list

to go

contact

Note

_____

_____

_____

_____

_____

_____

_____

DAILY PLANNERS

DATE

M	T	W	T	F	S	S

Inspiration

_____

_____

_____

_____

general plan	to do list

to go

contact

Note

_____

_____

_____

_____

_____

_____

_____

DAILY PLANNERS

DATE

M T W T F S S

Inspiration

general plan   to do list

to go

contact

Note

DAILY PLANNERS

DATE

M	T	W	T	F	S	S

Inspiration

_____

_____

_____

_____

general plan	to do list	

to go

contact

Note

_____

_____

_____

_____

_____

_____

_____

DAILY PLANNERS

DATE

M T W T F S S

Inspiration

_____

_____

_____

_____

general plan	to do list	

○ _____

○ _____   **to go**

○ _____

○ _____

○ _____

○ _____

○ _____

○ _____   **contact**

○ _____

○ _____

○ _____

Note

_____

_____

_____

_____

_____

_____

_____

DAILY PLANNERS

DATE

M	T	W	T	F	S	S

Inspiration

_____

_____

_____

_____

general plan	to do list

_____

_____

_____

_____

_____

_____

_____

_____

_____

_____

to go

contact

Note

_____

_____

_____

_____

_____

_____

_____

DAILY PLANNERS

DATE

M T W T F S S

Inspiration

_____

_____

_____

_____

general plan	to do list	

to go

contact

Note

_____

_____

_____

_____

_____

_____

_____

_____

DAILY PLANNERS

DATE

M	T	W	T	F	S	S

Inspiration

_____

_____

_____

_____

general plan	to do list

to go

contact

Note

_____

_____

_____

_____

_____

_____

_____

DAILY PLANNERS

DATE

M T W T F S S

Inspiration

_____

_____

_____

general plan	to do list	

to go

contact

Note

_____

_____

_____

_____

_____

_____

DAILY PLANNERS

DATE

M	T	W	T	F	S	S

Inspiration

_____

_____

_____

_____

general plan	to do list	

to go

contact

Note

_____

_____

_____

_____

_____

_____

_____

DAILY PLANNERS

DATE

M T W T F S S

Inspiration

_____

_____

_____

_____

general plan	to do list

_____

_____

_____

_____

_____

_____

_____

_____

_____

_____

_____

to go

contact

Note

_____

_____

_____

_____

_____

_____

_____

DAILY PLANNERS

DATE

M	T	W	T	F	S	S

Inspiration

_____

_____

_____

_____

general plan	to do list

to go

contact

Note

_____

_____

_____

_____

_____

_____

_____

_____

DAILY PLANNERS

DATE

M	T	W	T	F	S	S

Inspiration

_____

_____

_____

general plan	to do list

to go

contact

Note

_____

_____

_____

_____

_____

_____

_____

DAILY PLANNERS

DATE

M	T	W	T	F	S	S

Inspiration

_____
_____
_____
_____

general plan	to do list	

to go

contact

Note

_____
_____
_____
_____
_____
_____

DAILY PLANNERS

DATE

M T W T F S S

Inspiration

_____

_____

_____

_____

general plan	to do list	

to go

contact

Note

_____

_____

_____

_____

_____

_____

_____

DAILY PLANNERS

DATE

M	T	W	T	F	S	S

Inspiration

_____

_____

_____

_____

general plan	to do list

to go

contact

Note

_____

_____

_____

_____

_____

_____

_____

DAILY PLANNERS

DATE

M T W T F S S

Inspiration

_____

_____

_____

_____

general plan	to do list

to go

contact

Note

_____

_____

_____

_____

_____

_____

_____

_____

DAILY PLANNERS

DATE

M T W T F S S

Inspiration

_____
_____
_____
_____

| general plan | to do list |

to go

contact

Note

_____
_____
_____
_____
_____
_____
_____

DAILY PLANNERS

DATE

M	T	W	T	F	S	S

Inspiration

_____

_____

_____

_____

general plan   to do list

_____   ○ _____

_____   ○ _____

_____   ○ _____

to go

_____   ○ _____

_____   ○ _____

_____   ○ _____

_____   ○ _____

_____   ○ _____

contact

_____   ○ _____

_____   ○ _____

_____   ○ _____

Note

_____

_____

_____

_____

_____

_____

_____

DAILY PLANNERS

DATE

M	T	W	T	F	S	S

Inspiration

_____
_____
_____
_____

general plan	to do list	

to go

contact

Note

_____
_____
_____
_____
_____
_____
_____

DAILY PLANNERS

DATE

M	T	W	T	F	S	S

Inspiration

_____

_____

_____

general plan	to do list

to go

contact

Note

_____

_____

_____

_____

_____

_____

_____

DAILY PLANNERS

DATE

M	T	W	T	F	S	S

Inspiration
_____
_____
_____
_____

general plan	to do list	
		to go
		contact

Note
_____
_____
_____
_____
_____
_____
_____

DAILY PLANNERS

DATE

M	T	W	T	F	S	S

Inspiration

_____
_____
_____

general plan   to do list

_____   ◯_____   **to go**
_____   ◯_____
_____   ◯_____
_____   ◯_____
_____   ◯_____
_____   ◯_____
_____   ◯_____   **contact**
_____   ◯_____
_____   ◯_____
_____   ◯_____
_____   ◯_____

Note

_____
_____
_____
_____
_____
_____
_____

www.ingramcontent.com/pod-product-compliance
Lightning Source LLC
Chambersburg PA
CBHW080737250626
47170CB00010B/2859